HUMOROUS INCIDENTS, SHORT STORIES AND ESSAYS

Beach Towns, Politics of Everybody, and Government That Works

RAUF BOLDEN

Published by: VELVETILLUSION S. A.

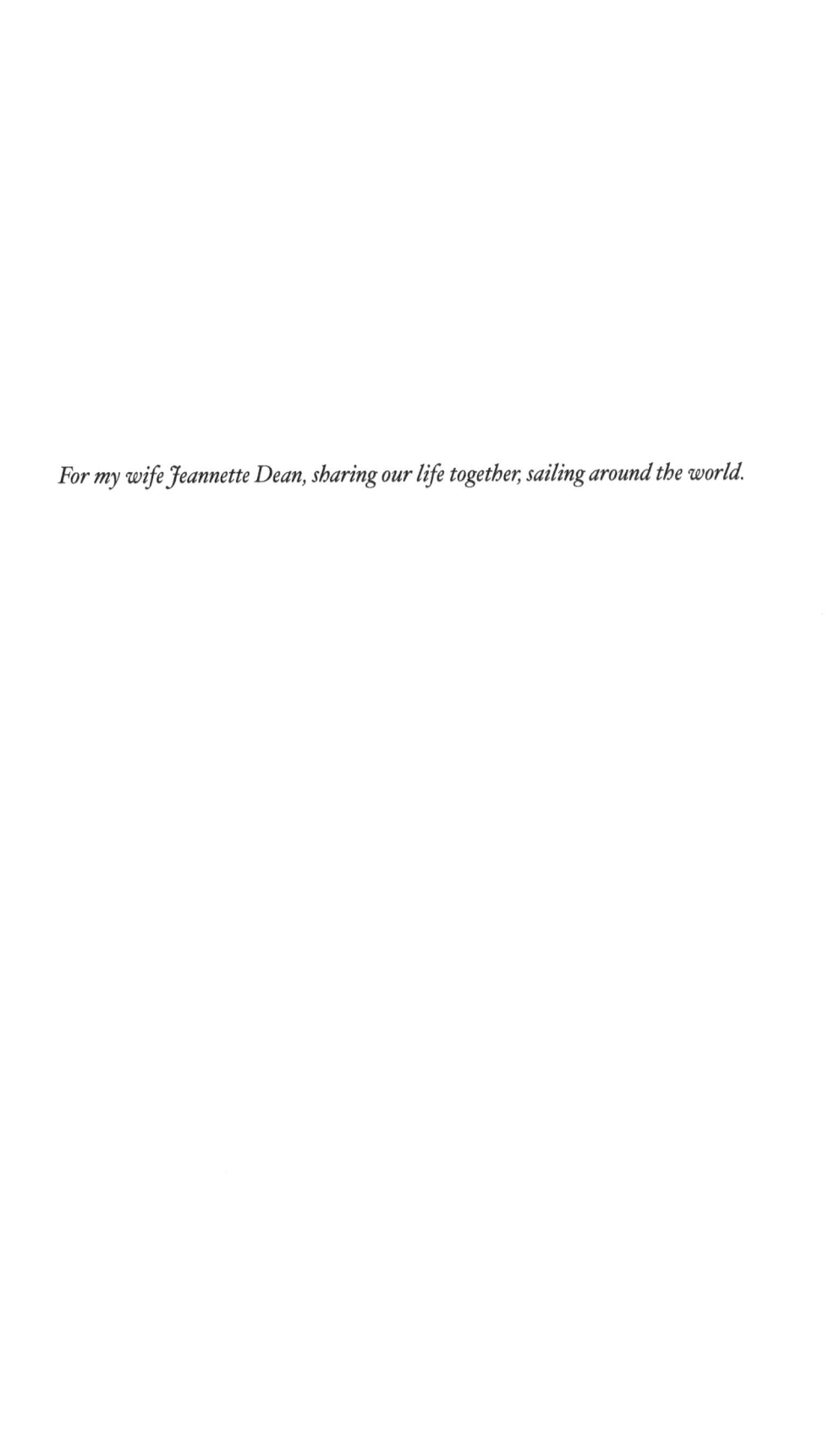

For my wife Jeannette Dean, sharing our life together, sailing around the world.

DISCLOSURE

The views, thoughts, and opinions expressed in the text belong solely to the author.

INTRODUCTION

Our tale is about Li'l Johny, as he wades through the literal and political swamp of south Alabama's peculiar politics of everybody, wandering from the wetlands to the beach, traversing the Backcountry Trail, bordered by the jurisdiction of the Orange Beach Government.

This collection of humorous incidents, short stories and essays provides a platform for addressing political points that local government has not, or is not willing to tackle like rebating the 4-mil property tax.

The plan is to make people aware that vast wealth is hidden in the vaults at City Hall ($40 Million in cash reserves), but the residents (population around: 5,600) are seeing no revenue sharing in their pockets. This situation is not a dark humor short story, but the sad reality of unbridled ambition.

The key issue is local government's sense of solutionism, meaning one vision is the best solution for everyone moving forward, possibly exporting the mayor's brand of leadership to all the beaches of the world as an example of pro-growth tourism.

Some people will argue the Orange Beach government has a vision. I refer you to this quote, "...load up and come to a council meeting so that u can get the facts, the real truth and stop being educated into further ignorance by following this site [Facebook]," posted by Orange Beach Mayor Tony Kennon on Facebook.

We are blessed in our country to have a voice, and with this voice I ask for a government that works, respecting other ideas without being called down in the Council Chambers. I argue for a chance to free Council Members from the yoke of always voting unanimously with the Mayor.

Perhaps Council Districting is the answer, forcing Council Members to live in the neighborhoods they represent, voting for their constituents' best interests instead of serving the city at-large. Perhaps we could ask Council Members to voluntarily share their personal and business tax returns, disclosing what development projects they, or their family members hold a financial interest in.

This is why we are here, creating a sense of financial transparency, and rebating a small portion of the city's wealth back to the residents.

HUMOROUS INCIDENTS, SHORT STORIES AND ESSAYS:

Beach Towns, Politics of Everybody, and Government that Works

By Rauf Bolden

LI'L JOHNY

Li'l Johny walked out of the convenience store at Buc-ees, heading towards the Foley Beach Express, looking forward to getting paid in Orange Beach.

It was about half a mile to the road before he could start hitch-hiking. He stuck out his thumb, immediately a car stopped.

"Are you a Republican or a Democrat?" the driver asked.

"I'm a Democrat," Li'l Johny replied.

Vroom the car sped off down the Expressway.

He scratched his head wondering what just happened. Li'l Johny threw his bedroll over his shoulder and kept walking.

The clouds were ominous, hovering in the west. It looked like a sign of rain.

Johny decided to try again, sticking out his thumb.

After several attempts another car stopped.

"Are you a Republican or a Democrat?" the driver asked.

"I'm a Democrat," Li'l Johny replied.

Vroom the car sped off down the Expressway.

Johny was confused as a light rain started to drizzle.

He stuck out his thumb again.

A beautiful lady pulled over, raising up the top on her convertible. Johny noticed her skirt sliding up her legs.

"Are you a Republican or a Democrat?" she asked.

"I'm a Republican," Li'l Johny replied.

"Get in," she said.

She drove fast. The skirt riding up and down her leg as she shifted.

Johny asked, "Why are you going to the beach?"

"I am going to a historical preservation conference. We have a condo at the Wharf, and the conference is at the Event Center across the road."

"What about you?" she asked.

"I never been to the Flora-Bama," he lied, thinking about getting paid. "It's on my bucket list."

Li'l Johny was caught up in the moment as they sped down the Expressway.

He thought, "I've been a Republican for ten minutes, and already I want to screw somebody."

❧ 2 ❧
EFFECTS OF HISTORY ON ORANGE BEACH

History is littered with politicians, kissing the ring-of-opportunity in public even as they roll their eyes in private, and so it is with the history of political opportunities that shaped our island.

Orange Beach's history started with a fish, according to oral historian Gail Walker, curator of the Indian and Sea Museum. Her ancestors were Creek Indians, having settled this area in the 1700s, founding the communities of Bear Point and Caswell. By the 1800s the idea of an orange beach germinated, prompting Gail's ancestors to plant orange-tree hybrids that were a cross between oranges and satsumas, beloved for their vibrant-orange color.

For Gail's ancestors the Civil War was about holding onto their land. Her great-grandfather Lemuel, being a full-blooded Creek Indian, enlisted in the Confederate Army in Ft. Morgan when he was 14 years old and marched to fight in Tennessee. He returned with two soldiers who later died from their musket-ball wounds. They are buried in the cemetery at Bear Point.

Lemuel rode his horse to Washington, DC, securing a land deed for $200, signed by President Lincoln. The Creeks in Ft. Morgan somehow avoided the Trail-of-Tears March to Oklahoma when the

Federal Government rounded up the Indian Tribes in Alabama after the Civil War.

The 1900s saw change. Gail's father was born in 1910 in Caswell, inheriting his family's turpentine business, milking the local trees for their sap, collecting it in barrels, and sailing it to Mobile where the pitch was converted into turpentine.

Her relatives also owned and operated the old Orange Beach Hotel. It consisted of hand-made bricks on the walkways and in the chimney, being destroyed in 2015 to create the Coastal Arts Center.

Gail's family were fisherman, founding the island's charter-fishing business when a chance encounter with a tourist in 1956 sent them offshore, landing a sailfish onboard a small boat, becoming the economic driver that it is today.

Building on the rich history we inherited requires caring, because the history of the people is also a history of the island's ecology. Hurting one hurts the other.

We are at a point in the economic-growth cycle where roads, population and infrastructure have more political bandwidth than protecting the environment, because we are taxing natural resources in a way we cannot reconcile. This level of development has never happened before. We do not know the consequences of continued approved-by-right construction on the beach.

Gail Walker's ancestors fought to hold onto their land. In different ways the ownership of property is as precious to us today. Instead of acreage, it is development on the beach. The slices of ownership are smaller than a 1700s land hold, but the desire for ownership is part of the human spirit.

With Gail's ancestors, the stress on the land was less, and that is the key issue. The City is satisfying the developers' desire for property ownership through planned-unit-developments, creating more intensity per acre than the beach has ever had before.

Mayor Tony Kennon told Fox10 News, "You can't stop the growth. It's coming whether you like it or not." Trying to find ways to create more developments, the chin strokers proceed, scratching it like a suppurating wound, finding the gray area, moving the goal posts, browbeating the opposition into quiescence. Expecting anything different is hope over reality.

Saying you can't stop the growth, but at the same time voting to ban short-term house rentals in the neighborhoods with minimal-environmental impact is troubling, voting against the business interests of smalltime-property investors, voting against families who rent their properties for income, voting against families' rights to seek financial improvement through property rentals, voting against customers' rights to choose between a condo on the beach or a house in the neighborhoods is troubling.

I digress. Purchasing a large stretch of beach for Orange Beach residents to enjoy with their families, reducing the environmental impact, increasing happiness, making a better quality of life for the locals who live here is something Council needs to do. Once in a generation, politicians become leaders, assisting in the development of an affluent, safe, and debt-free city with a beautiful beach. Piloted by captains who want to achieve a sense of well-being for their people. Grasping that opportunity is another matter.

❧ 3 ❧

POWER LINE ROAD

Li'l Johny got up early, leaving the condo. She was expecting her husband and kids around noon.

He stopped for coffee and croissant at the Southern Grind, walking with his backpack and bed roll, headed for Power Line Road. It's a known couch surfer route to the beach.

Johny crossed Canal Road, coming to the short cut. It used to be the direct road to the beach, but now it was never used. The government settled the Deep Water Horizon Oil Spill in exchange for no development across the State Park for twenty years.

It was a couple of miles to the old Wireman house, nestled by a little pond. Johny settled down under some trees reading his Kindle.

He awoke when cars drove up. It was dark. Their lights were off. Johny grabbed his stuff and slid around the back of the house so he could see through the window.

They only used flashlights, moving along the wall.

A squawking voice broke the night, "I see you and Jesus sees you too."

They killed the flashlights.

Again, the squawking voice, "I see you and Jesus sees you too."

One of the group turned on a flashlight and shined it around the room, landing on a cage with a parrot inside.

He visibly exhaled saying. "You're just a parrot."

The squawking voice answered, "And Jesus is the Rottweiler."

Johny took off running toward the state park, hearing the commotion from the house. He ran, and ran, and ran until he fell against a small oak tree. He climbed, using his belt as a tether, securing himself to a branch and slept.

REJECTING ENVIRONMENTALISM
IN ORANGE BEACH

The construction of the new Lodge in the Alabama State Park set the bar, specifying solar panels for power, recycling water from air conditioners, catching rainwater off the roof, and innovating in ways that reflect the environmental values of our local community. The Gulf State Park Lodge is a shining example, begging our local elected officials to wake up and smell the coffee.

Environmentally friendly technologies like solar panels; air conditioner water recycling and rainwater collection are viable, being easily incorporated into building sustainable technologies for the new Middle School/High School in Orange Beach. Unfortunately, the political will is not there.

By contrast, "The park is recognized as an international benchmark for environmental and economic sustainability," according to a report on Gulf State Park Facebook Page.

Broadening the sustainability equation, enveloping the City of Orange Beach will help the city's environmental image, simultaneously generating significant energy and water savings over time, re-paying the initial cost of adding renewable systems to the new school's construction. The Gulf State Park is leading the way.

The Lodge's sustainability profile provides an impressive example to follow:

"It [the Lodge] collects, stores and treats 105 percent of the water needed by guests and the surrounding landscape. It features an 11,000-gallon water cistern that stores rainwater collected from the building's roof. It [the Lodge] is completely self-sufficient and will generate 105 percent of the power needed with solar panels placed at the site's southwest corner (This means the facility generates more energy than it uses.)," according to a report on Gulf State Park Facebook.

I argue, mandating FORTIFIED Homes and Commercial be built as energy and water efficient as they are hurricane resistant is crucial, minimizing the environmental impact on Orange Beach.

How did we get here?

"Hurricane Ivan made landfall in Gulf Shores on September 16, 2004 and devastated [the] Gulf State Park. This category III storm (categorized as one of the top five worst storms to make landfall on the Gulf Coast) broke the pier into three sections, washed out the bottom floors of the hotel, totaled one of the cabins, and flooded the majority of the park with salt water," according to a report on Alabama State Parks web site.

Ivan required Orange Beach to re-evaluate new home and commercial builds, adopting the FORTIFIED Homes and Commercial criteria as their building codes, but no environmental sustainability amendments like solar panels and water recycling were included.

"We [The State Park Lodge] meet the highest standards for an environmentally sustainable hospitality and meeting experience and are seeking certification as a LEED Gold facility, FORTIFIED Commercial facility, and SITES Platinum landscape," according to a report on The Lodge's web site.

"With new trailheads and places to pause, along with interpretive and wayfinding [sic] signage along the way, it's ideal for enjoying the stunning natural beauty of Alabama's Gulf Coast. And it's accessible to all levels of physical ability. So, park your car and leave it behind for unforgettable hikes of all types," according to a report on The Gulf State Park web site.

What appears to be environmental harmony in Orange Beach like trails and clean beaches makes the symphony incomplete without interconnected sustainability woven into the fabric of our local building codes.

The City of Orange Beach is singularly focused on the big picture, primarily its bottom line. The FORTIFIED Homes and Commercial standard provide reductions in insurance premiums for locals; but environmental sustainability does not.

Mayor Tony Kennon came away impressed with the new lodge, and its stout construction. "I think they did a first-class job," Kennon said in a report in the Lagniappe. "It's a unique design but it's also built in such a way to be fortified to withstand storms and survive. So, I'm very proud of it."

He never disappoints, clearly implying FORTIFIED Homes and Commercial standards are important to him. I argue for a plan, demanding resource conservation measures like solar power and water recycling be incorporated into the city's FORTIFIED Homes and Commercial building codes, as environmental addendums.

When the Gulf State Park opened, the speeches were a master class on the Park's aspirations for the local community. Mayor Kennon entertained his friends, clearly not cheerleading these sustainability standards. I assume it was because there is no financial incentive in it for him.

A solar powered house in Orange Beach does not add more money into the city's general fund from the electrical cooperative's partnership with local government. Every year Baldwin EMC presents the City Council with a check for approximately $1 Million, from coal generated power sold to local residents.

Alternatively, the Gulf State Park's sustainability statement suggests raising the standard of environmental ethics over monetary gain, "Environmentally friendly operations and facilities; support for the protection of cultural and natural heritage; direct and tangible social and economic benefits to local people," according to a report on The Lodge at Gulf State Park web site.

On the face of it, Baldwin EMC and Orange Beach rail against adding solar homes and commercial, because it cuts into their margins.

According to documentation obtained in an email from Greg

Gipson, Manager of Business Development, Energy Services, and Advanced Metering at Baldwin EMC, the electrical provider requires liability insurance and upgrade-payment guarantees from EMC's solar customers. This procedure insulates EMC's upstream suppliers from financial exposure by pushing additional expenses for solar connectivity down onto the solar users, according to EMC's "Members Guide to Interconnected Distributed Resource", pgs. 8-9.

"The Member (read: EMC customer) may be compensated for the power [on solar projects] that flows onto the distribution system," according to EMC's "Members Guide to Interconnected Distribution", pg. 7. This language is conspicuously vague as to if and how much credit is given for each watt of solar power generated.

The city's position is diametrically opposed to the environmental values espoused by the Alabama Gulf State Park. The Park calls for, "Direct and tangible social and economic benefits to local people," according to a report on The Lodge at Gulf State Park web site.

Elected officials in Orange Beach made a conscious choice about climate change, solar power, and water recycling by not following the State Park's example. Instead of insisting the new Middle School/High School be constructed using revised FORTIFIED Homes and Commercial building codes, running on solar power with recycled water as a precedent for sustainability, the Council decided to spend tens-of-millions on ball fields, and a performing-arts center, powered in the traditional way, perhaps by coal-fired power plants. It is an opportunity lost, affecting generations to come.

5

NATALIE

Li'l Johny slept in the dunes close to the Gulf State Park, ensuring no one was after him. He emerged in the early morning, making his way across the Beach Road.

He sat at a table near the window, overlooking the beach, and ordered coffee. The literature from the front desk described in detail the lengths the State Park went to, ensuring environmental sustainability in their signature beach project.

The server came by. He asked, "Is Natalie here?"

"She only works evenings. Come back after six."

He returned around nine, having showered at the outside facility on the beach.

"Table for one the hostess asked?"

"I'll sit at the bar."

"What can I get you?" Her name tag reads Natalie.

"Natalie, I want to see if you can mix me a really good martini."

"Coming right up."

"And make one for yourself too," he said.

She smiled and grabbed two glasses.

Li'l Johny had a meal, drinking with Natalie, leaving her a hundred-dollar bill after each round.

"Are you always this generous," she asked.

"No, but you are special."

She invited him back to her place, overlooking the white sand beach, spending the night in each other's arms.

Li'l Johny returned the next night around nine.

"Table for one the hostess asked?"

"I'll sit at the bar."

Natalie asked, "What can I get you?"

"I will start with martinis if you'll join me."

"Can do," she said, setting up two glasses. "You know I never thought I'd see you again."

"I am not a one-night stand guy."

He had a meal, leaving her a hundred-dollar bill after each round.

They went back to her place, waking in the morning she asked, "Do you travel all the time?"

"I just came back from Medellin, Colombia."

"I have a sister in Medellin."

"I know she gave me a few thousand dollars for you."

❦ 6 ❧

CALL FOR PURCHASING A PUBLIC BEACH

B uying beachfront property for the greater good of Orange Beach residents is not in sync with local government's views of spending money without a verifiable return-on-investment. A gated beach with ample parking and bathroom facilities for the residents is obviously frivolous compared to Council's aggressive investment criteria, but it does meet the criteria of local voters, caring very much to have a place in the sun for their families to enjoy.

It is as if elected officials are undervaluing their electoral alliances. They are not seeing the happiness they could generate with the local voters through this simple act of community good, giving residents something constituent families can actually touch besides a bridge.

The problem of providing public access to beaches baffles policy experts across the country.

"An increase in the population of coastal counties and popularity of coastal beaches as tourism destinations create difficulties for management agencies responsible for providing public beach access," according to a report in Science Direct.

Orange Beach has three public beaches, owned and maintained by the State of Alabama, according to a report by Gulf Shores & Alabama Tourism.

The city does not own a beach, compared to Gulf Shores with expansive public beach, being large enough to hold the Hangout Music Festival (35,000 people).

Mayor Tony Kennon heralds the natural beauty of our privately-owned beaches, but is loath to endorse the purchase of dedicated-beach access for local residents, having kept a controlling hand on the treasury for the past decade.

"While you [tourists] are here, you will come to understand what we mean by this ['Life is better here'] as you soak in the spectacular beauty of our sunrises, sunsets and enjoy walking along our sandy white beaches [property of hotels or condos]," wrote Mayor Tony Kennon on the city's web site.

Imagine a gated beach with membership card access, scanning in like we do at the Recreation Center. Even planning a presentation of this idea is made difficult, because Orange Beach does not have a finance committee that is open to the public, allowing citizens to sign-up, submitting spending ideas to the Mayor for consideration during his budget process. Suggesting government and residents have a shared political consciousness is mistaken; coordinated planning is easier said than done.

Some argue beaches should not be owned at all.

"Beach access is a universal right and necessary for the public's enjoyment of the beach," according to a report on Beachapedia.

"The public should be afforded full and fair access to beaches, which are public trust resources, by minimizing the possibility of impediment; including development, subdivision or land use zoning change; or deterring obstacles, including gates, fences, hired security, misleading signage, rock walls, shrubbery or other blockades, being placed upon public rights of way to beach access," according to a report on the environmental website Surfrider.

Orange Beach has a responsibility to its citizens for safety, and protection, certainly providing beach access does not fall under these parameters. The idea of providing beach access for future generations to enjoy is nice since Orange Beach can afford it, but it does not fall under the umbrella of public safety.

That is the problem, convincing Mayor Kennon that an important element in life is sharing with your neighbors, increasing the quality of life for the residents, foregoing running the city like a business, because the city is a tax-free entity as it is.

If the $40 million Orange Beach has in reserves were taxed it would only be $25 million, so use $25 million to better the quality of life for the people who live here by purchasing a stretch of beach for residents to use.

I have heard employees say, it is easier to get the truth out of the White House than it is to get lunch money out of Mayor Tony Kennon.

Our mayor's fiscal policies are rewriting the laws of political frugality, but unlike conservatives who are constantly conscience of their cheering base, our mayor is greeted with cautious, measured skepticism from the opposition and shrugged shoulders from those on the fence.

Admittedly our mayor's supporters stand shoulder-to-shoulder with his brand of fiscal conservatism, concerning a beach for residents.

"I want to know the cost before making any decision," said Bill Jeffries, Planning Commissioner, and 12-year resident of Orange Beach.

"Not needed [beach access]! I'm working toward another bridge for Orange Beach," said Alan McElroy, retired businessman, and longtime resident.

"Cut out the dang foolishness and build a boat launch at the pass. We already have three beaches, owned by the State," purred Cecil Young, Board-of-Adjustment member, and lifetime resident of Orange Beach.

Arguing a double standard exists, because of the beach mouse habitat that ostensibly blocked the proposed boat launch near the pass Cecil Young added, "It didn't worry them about the beach mouse when they built the condos, so why should they worry about it when they're building a boat ramp?"

Obviously, the choir does not lack voices, singing for disbursement of the same pot of money.

Residents who get up and go to work in the morning feel trapped in a cut-throat economy of food service jobs and stagnant wages, wanting to have a sanctuary, experiencing a little sun, having a few laughs by going to an uncrowded beach with their families. Once done a residents' beach is forever.

❄ 7 ❄

YOUTUBER

Li'l Johny left the beach, impressed the trash was always picked up, and headed across the dunes to the Backcountry Trail.

He came across a mini camp site, watching a family from the woods. The children were holding a snake, sneaking up on one of the tents. The called and a head emerged, facing the snake.

Screams started and struggles to get out of the tent.

The children were laughing.

Li'l Johny wake up and asked what happened.

"Our brother is always playing jokes on us and we finally got even.

Johny followed the map to the small pavilion. He sat in the enclosure, sheltered from the bugs. The children from the camp site arrived on their bicycles. The brother was with them. One of the kids pulled out a phone, showing him the video.

"Is it on YouTube already?"

❧ 8 ❧

ECOTOURISM AS ECONOMIC STIMULUS IN ORANGE BEACH

For many years, I have assured people that it is easy to be an expert on Orange Beach because there are really only two answers to any question you could ever be asked about it: "I don't know" and "It depends." While glib, this point is strikingly accurate. The public face of Orange Beach's council system is highly transparent with meetings and work sessions in a public forum. Its inner workings and decision-making processes are shrouded in mystery, wondering about who is really making the decisions, rarely conforming to what any outsider might predict. Perhaps ecotourism's economic value to this community is the galvanizing exception, making it priceless.

"Ecotourism is considered the fastest growing market in the tourism industry," according to the World Tourism Organization with an annual growth rate of 5% worldwide and representing 6% of the world's gross domestic product, 11.4% of all consumer spending, bolstering local economies.

Behavioral economists combine economics with insights from psychology to show how heavily economic decisions like ecotourism are influenced by cognitive biases, according to the Economist Magazine's summary of Richard Thaler's work. He is the winner of this

year's Nobel Prize in Economics. According to him our economic decisions are influenced by cognitive biases like ecotourism, influencing
our decision to choose vacation cities that are eco-friendly.

Environmental tourism began in Orange Beach after the Great
Depression of 2008, being an inadvertently disguised format for
economic stimulus, injecting government funds into the economy,
bolstering the recovery, as John Maynard Keynes espoused.

The City wrote grants to build the Backcountry Trail System,
continually encouraging investment in offshore fisheries with artificial
reefs and scuba diving, having ships demolished as underwater attrac-
tions, extending the red-snapper fishing season, using cognitive biases,
ensuring vacationers understood we are pro-environment, promoting
growth in the local economy.

A Beach Ambassador Initiative was started. "Leave Only Foot-
prints," affects all aspects of beach life, erasing tents, chairs and para-
phernalia from the beach at night, presenting a fresh canvas each
morning for our visitors to enjoy, creating jobs in the economy.

These emissaries had a busy season in 2016: Public Interactions:
51,124; Promotional Items Distributed: 20,439; Glass Warnings Issued:
3322; Tent Warnings Issued: 3285; Tents Tagged: 886; Hole Warnings:
1378; Holes Filled: 2170; Trash Warnings: 485; Trash Bags Distributed:
5689; Law Enforcement (Backup) Requests: 46; Fire/EMS/Rescue
Requests: 14; Dog Issues/Encounters: 157; Wildlife Related Incidents:
88; Metal Shovel Warnings: 71, according to a representative from
Orange Beach Coastal Resources in an email.

Investing in ecotourism as a form of economic stimulus has
strengthened economic growth in Orange Beach through active partic-
ipation by our tourism partners: Alabama Department of Environmental Management, The Citizen and Visitors Bureau, The Orange
Beach Chamber-of-Commerce, The Backcountry Trail Foundation,
The Islands of Perdido Foundation, The Alabama Coastal Foundation
and the Fishing Association, providing sustainable-business examples
to build on.

Perhaps economic stimulus was not the root concept of the initial
plan, supporting ecotourism from the beach initiative to turtle nesting,
but economic stimulus was certainly the end result.

The trails network, beach ambassadorship, turtle nesting, trash pickups on the islands, dredging the pass for offshore-fishing access, increasing the red-snapper season require complex management skills and grant-writing abilities, rewarded when driven from the perspective that infrastructure stimulus creates jobs in the local economy.

Businesses profit from ecotourism. Being seen to be caring for and taking care of the environment is behavioral economics, supporting initiatives for Beach Mouse habitat; tag-and-release fishing; rental of bicycles, pontoon boats, and jet skis; or going on Segway tours, is making an environmental statement to our visitors, underlining the council's commitment to Orange Beach's eco-friendly image.

Finding the funds for these projects is key; writing grants is not a funding source one can depend on year-in-and-year-out. The City of Orange Beach recently increased the Lodging Tax by 2% from 11% to 13%, generating $5 Million per year in additional revenue, according to Finance Director Ford Handley. One assumes some of these funds will be allocated to stabilize ecotourism's infrastructure budget.

The Backcountry-Trail Tours yielded: 408 tours and 1869 visitors, divided by the number of years since inception is 208 visitors per year. On tour, visitors learn the inter-dependency between flora and fauna indigenous to the Gulf Coast. This educational approach diversifies the offerings available to visitors in Orange Beach.

Turtle nesting is also an important component, watching the beach during the summer months, patrolling at night with teams of volunteers, looking for females coming ashore, burying their eggs in the sand. Volunteers protect the nesting sites with markers, patiently waiting for the hatchlings to surface, escorting them to the sea, ensuring the survival of another generation.

Environmental projects like these require funding to continue. The City of Orange Beach has shown no sign of curbing its appetite for allocating resources, presenting a unified face with everyone in step, assuring council remains proud of the city's eco-friendly image.

Some holdouts still exist, citing "disputable findings about climate change", quoting the new Director of the Environmental Protection Agency, Scott Pruitt. "I would not agree that carbon dioxide is a primary contributor to the global warming that we see," he told CNBC's "Squawk Box."

President Trump's position on environmental protection "has been consistent," Environmental Defense Fund President Fred Krupp notes in an essay published in the July-August issue of *Foreign Affairs*, a subscribers-only magazine. "He wants far less of it," according to their blog.

Therefore, the constituents of Orange Beach must follow their own compass, because Federal Grants for environmental projects are diminishing.

Orange Beach's approximate 5,600 residents are a tiny microcosm in the greater scope of the nation, manning their own tiller, implementing their own style of environmental ethics, riding the wave of ecotourism to stimulate the local economy, gladly pulling together with all-hands-on-deck towards a common-ecological goal, because ecotourism's economic value to this community is priceless.

❦ 9 ❦

SAVOIR FAIRE

L i'l Johny found an oak tree behind the butterfly garden that was low and simple to climb. He hooked his rock climbing sleeping tent to an upper limb, and went to sleep.

In the morning he cleaned up in the pavilion's bathrooms, setting out towards City Hall.

"Good morning," she said. Her name tag reads Sugar. She offered coffee and pastries, probably the best customer service presentation he had ever experienced.

"I'd like to see the Mayor," Li'l Johny replied.

"Do you have an appointment?"

"No, I'll wait."

"He's in meetings right now. We have a Council Meeting tonight," she said. "It may be awhile."

Li'l Johny sat in the lobby, listening to two French journalists explaining to their guide the meaning of *savoir faire*.

"Imagine when you come home and find your daughter in bed with her boyfriend," one said. "You say carry on and close the door. That is *savoir faire*."

"Non," said the other in heavily accented English. "Imagine when you come home and find your daughter in bed with her boyfriend. You say carry on, grabbing a chair you sit down. If he can carry on, that is *savoir faire*.

❧ 10 ❧

HOW TO RUN FOR MAYOR AND COUNCIL

G etting elected Mayor or to the City Council in 2020 is simple.

Campaign on a platform to eliminate the 4-mil property tax, giving residents a real return for putting up with the traffic, and propose we pay for the tax cut with sin taxes on tobacco products, alcohol, and sugary drinks, offsetting the money lost on the tax cut. This oversimplification sounds easy, but it's not.

Orange Beach has competent council members, being skilled politicians, representing their community on an at-large basis, not districts. Jeff Silvers and Joni Blalock have served the longest since 2004; Jerry Johnson and Jeff Boyd have served since 2012; Annette Mitchell was appointed to serve out the term of the late Al Bradley, being elected to her first term in 2016.

Mayor Tony Kennon started out as a Councilman, being first elected on August 24, 2004, but resigned on June 7, 2005. Three years later, on August 26, 2008 he was elected Mayor, presently serving his third consecutive term, ending in 2020.

To qualify for the ballot, you have to meet a few minimum requirements. The candidate "must be 18 years old; must be a resident of the city for 90 days prior to the election [rent or own]; must be a US citizen for one day; and must be a registered voter," according to a report on the Alabama Secretary of State's website.

Planning your run for the 2020 election cycle takes time and hard work, beginning in 2019. Start building up a war chest of donor lists, appropriate technology and talented volunteers.

How do you go about getting elected to public office? Here are a few pointers.

Know your electorate: talk with people across the entire economic spectrum, finding out what matters to them; connect with bellwethers, getting the right people backing you; kick off fundraising by contacting past candidates; build your team, knowing volunteers will do the bulk of the work; design campaign material, concentrating on poster and yard sign design, newsletters, and social media. Raise candidate's profile, reaching out to voters through common acquaintances. Create a campaign plan for messaging and build a dedicated voter database, tracking communication through websites, social media and telephone calls, according to a report on CallHub, a political website.

Offending one person with your campaign style in a small town may mean offending their entire voting family. Note that council members are sometimes elected with as little as 400 votes. In 2008 Tony Kennon had around 1200 votes, being elected mayor in a town of 5000 people.

The margin for offending is large, but the margin for winning is small, adding to that, the responsibility for winning is enormous, putting you on-call 24/7 for a low-paying job.

"I know when my Dad [Councilman Jerry Davidson] was on council [2000-2004] he spent an enormous amount time in many more meetings [council planning] than the public meetings held and people took any and all opportunities anytime he was anywhere to discuss their thoughts," said Kristy Doggett a twenty-year resident in an email.

Some people cannot be bothered with public service, saying it is too much trouble, putting up with all the politics for a beggar's wage: $13,401.18 per year for each council member; $16,557.36 per year for the Mayor Pro-Tem (vice-mayor); and $42,000.00 per year for Mayor.

Then there is the question of getting along with Mayor Kennon (if re-elected), having a very unique style of coordinating policy. Potential candidates muse about the fringe benefit of being embarrassed and humiliated in the Council Chambers for disagreeing with him.

Baldwin County District Representative Daniel Catlin, who was standing in for Congressman Bradley Byrne at his congressional town hall, watched as Mayor Kennon attempted to demean, disgrace and shame Congressman Byrne's supporters in the Council Chambers.

"They [residents] are ignorant by choice," said Mayor Kennon, as evidenced in this video report from Cliff McCollum of Gulf Coast News Today.

The video speaks volumes.

We need a hefty selection of good candidates in 2020, offering a salary commensurate with the job's responsibilities, specifically large enough to compensate professionals for managing a $40 million budget. I suggest $160,000 per year for Mayor, and $50,000 per year for each of the five council members, as outlined in my previous article.

People in Orange Beach can do better than having their Mayor and City Council stand unopposed for municipal elections because of the low pay. Let's improve the compensation package for our elected officials, simultaneously attracting a large pool of candidates, showing the world democracy, and competitive elections have a strong tradition in Orange Beach.

✻ II ✻

ALLIGATOR

L'l Johny walked into the council chamber. They were already in session.

It seemed strange to him, because the king in the movies always sits in the center of the podium, but in this case the Mayor sat off to the side, producing an uneven focus.

Li'l Johny got on the Free WiFi and pulled up the agenda.

"We have an appeal for permit denial," said the Mayor.

There was a ruckus at the back of the room. Heads turn.

A man was walking down the aisle with a four-foot long alligator on a leash.

"What is going on here," demanded the Mayor.

"Sally here is crucial to my business, and I wanted to show you."

He took out a small bat and hit the alligator over the head.

She sat up like a dog and he tossed treats to her.

Then he made hand signals and she rolled over and played dead.

"This is easy to do," he said. "Asking the audience if anyone would like to try.

A voice came from the back

"I would, just don't hit me over the head as hard as you did that alligator."

12

ORANGE BEACH IS THE MUNICIPAL LEADER PROVIDING FREE WI-FI

Orange Beach has Free Wi-Fi at every city building, obviously excluding Police and Fire. This high-bandwidth service is free of charge for the public to use, and is available on a 24/7 basis. How did this happen?

In 2005 during reconstruction after Hurricane Ivan, former Mayor Steve Russo asked me if we could build a Wi-Fi blanket over the entire City of Orange Beach. Technologically it was not possible at that time.

Three years later, I met with Finance Committee Chairman Al Bradley, discussing IT budgets. He asked about innovation. I told him about the old mayor's idea of Wi-Fi as a public service. He liked the concept, but suggested the city provide free Wi-Fi at all city buildings instead of competing with the local providers for home service.

I knew we could make this happen, and increase employee productivity at the same time, but we needed to upgrade the city's technology infrastructure from copper to fiber-optic. As a lawyer and CPA Bradley understood. He retired as CEO of a company that used fiber optics, and he was able to get the funding a Chairman of the Finance Committee.

Al and City Attorney Wanda Cochran founded the Telecommunications Committee. We started work, monitoring Franchise Agreements for utility vendors digging up the city's rights-of-way. This tactic allowed us to strategically place the city's fiber-optic infrastructure. In the early days there were only three of us, but our brief quickly expanded to membership from almost every department in the city.

Projects of this size need to be done in multi-year steps. This is how it started.

We sought a fiber-optic partner with experience providing reliable high-speed service. I wrote a Request For Proposal (RFP), detailing the specifications, including four strands of dark fiber (dedicated for city use), owned by the City of Orange Beach. We also required sufficient bandwidth that would carry the city well into the future. Harbor Communications LLC (https://www.harborcom.com/) of Mobile won the bid, providing the infrastructure and the bandwidth.

Phase One:

- •City Hall
- •Finance
- •Fire Admin and Fire Station One
- •Police and Municipal Court
- •Library

Phase Two:

- •Senior Center
- •Art Center
- •Fire Station Two
- •Recreation Center
- •Tennis Center
- •Community Center
- •Aquatic Center

Phase Three:

- •Golf Center
- •Sportsplex
- •Event Center

- •Sail Camp
- •Fire Station Five

Phase Four:

- •Public Works
- •Public Works Shop
- •Sewer Maintenance Shop
- •Sewer Plant

Planning for security was important. We resolved the public/private network issue, requiring each building have a physical separation (by external IP), rather than logical separation (by internal IP), segregating the networks from each other. This is more expensive, requiring additional hardware, but isolates each network on its own external IP address, eliminating the possibility of cross talk or network jumping.

Funding any municipal project is always a key issue. Al Bradley secured funding for the fiber-optic project as Chairman of the Finance Committee, and as Chairman of the Telecommunications Committee.

We presented a persuasive argument, stating fiber-optic connections also increased productivity for city workers. Image you are on a slow connection, spending ten minutes per day on DSL, drinking coffee, waiting for files to upload or download. This translates to 50 minutes per week, times 52 weeks per year, equals 2,600 minutes, or 43 hours (approx. one week) of productivity lost per year, per employee at each workstation. What business can afford that?

Some council members resisted, holding we do not need technological expansion, during a recession, combined with city-employee layoffs. With 20/20 hindsight, looking back to 2008 Chairman Al Bradley was a visionary, fighting to give all city offices the high-speed functionality needed for payment processing, jail bookings, event registrations, fire reporting, webinars, cameras, and online training, with the added amenity of Free Wi-Fi for the public to use. By leveraging the technology, we were able to demonstrate our solution; doing more with fewer employees is possible.

Orange Beach can thank one man for setting the bar so high for fiber-optic connectivity, allowing our city workers to be more efficient, simultaneously giving the public free access to high-speed Internet at city facilities.

This public service is invaluable, allowing residents to stream music as they work out in the gym, or for baseball parents to stream movies, waiting at the Sportsplex for their game to start. You can easily pull presentation files from your cloud account in the city's various meeting rooms, or download homework assignments after school. Orange Beach also provides the SEC and NAIA with bandwidth for broadcasting Women's Soccer Tournaments.

Al Lawton Bradley, Jr. (1950-2014) established the Free Wi-Fi standard in Orange Beach. This is a guiding light for other municipalities to follow.

✖ 13 ✖

OPENING STATEMENT

L i'l John left the Council Meeting, heading across the street to the woods behind the Police Station, finding a sprawling oak with lots of branches to hang his climbing ledge.

In the morning he would see how the court gained revenue instead of spending tax money.

He left his gear in the woods, having been warned the Police had heavy security at the court. Li'l Johny went through the metal detector and sat at the back on the aisle.

The Judge announced there would be no talking in his courtroom and banged the gavel.

After a couple of minutes, he pointed to a group sitting on the side and said, "You come up here and give the lady fifty dollars. I said no talking in my courtroom." Silence followed.

The Court Clerk called another case.

"What do you have to say for yourself," the Judge asked the defendant.

"It is all very simple your Honor and I can explain. You see I was sitting at the bar having my usual and in comes a frog."

"The frog sat next to me and I bought him a drink."

"We talked about the usual stuff, including sports and girls."

"It was getting late so I told the frog I was leaving."

He said, "I'm new in town and don't have a place to stay."

"My wife is out of town. You can come sleep on the couch."

We get to the house and I ask the frog if he's like a nightcap.

"After the drink, he asks me for a kiss."

"No one was there so I gave the frog a kiss, and poof the frog turns into that pile of dope you have in the corner," he said. "And that's my opening statement your Honor."

❧ 14 ❧

TAX CUTS

Tax cuts are Republican doctrine. Mayor Tony Kennon does not agree.

He raised the lodging tax from 11% to 13%, expressed mathematically it is a monetary increase of 15.38%, $(1.00 - 11/13) \times 100 = 15.38\%$. This Ordinance passed in the Council Chambers with five affirmative votes, only Councilman Jeff Boyd dissented.

Why are we gouging families who come to the beach on vacation?

The lodging tax is geared toward one goal, providing enough funding to build the Wolf Bay Bridge ($60 Million), ostensibly alleviating traffic, making life less stressful for everyone. "It took me 55 minutes to get home [from work], and I live ten miles away," said Lizzy Burch, Manager of Infinity Bicycles on Hwy. 161.

Even before the lodging increase, the city had over $40 million in reserves, generating $15 million above yearly expenses, according to financial reports on the city's web site. Mayor Kennon's logic is business centric, getting someone else to pay for the bridge through increased lodging taxes, thereby keeping his reserves in the vault.

Tax revenue is the life force of a municipality. Let's explore other ways Mayor Tony Kennon could generate income. Adding two cents to the gasoline tax at the local level, adding thirty cents to the cost of each sugary drink sold as a youth-targeted health tax, adding fifty cents to tobacco products is obviously a health tax, adding fifty cents to each alcoholic drink purchased in the bars and restaurants is a sin tax. All these would increase revenue, but would kill economic growth.

Is the role of government to increase revenue streams like a business, or stimulate economic growth?

John Maynard Keynes (1883-1946) defined tax cuts as a way to stimulate economic growth. In turn the growth from tax cuts pays for infrastructure like bridges. This concept is the foundation of creating wealth, heralded by Republicans as a pillar of conservative thought.

George W. Bush (R), and Donald J. Trump (R) pushed through tax cuts during their administrations. Mayor Tony Kennon (R) just doesn't get it. He espouses, I am running this city like a business, putting tax revenue ahead of economic growth.

A government is not a business. Firstly, a city is a tax-free entity, competing with a tax-free advantage. To manage a government like a business is opening oneself up to charges of leveraging the city's tax-free status, influencing vendors, cronyism, abuse of power, and ethical foul play.

If the city were a business, beholding to its shareholders, they would behave differently. The residents in Orange Beach have not had a direct return on their investment (ROI) in the last ten years, exposing the duplicity of the city's increasing revenues while living tax free, and not paying a dividend.

Let's look at it as a business. Tax cuts are a way to provide a return, but how?

Property tax repeal (4-mils) is a good place to start. In confidence, a Councilman once told me we need that money from property taxes, because they generate approximately $3.5 million per year in revenue. Taking $3.5 million out of a $40 million pot does not seem like a lot to me.

Going back to the words of John Maynard Keynes, cutting taxes spurs growth. We must have imagination. Eliminating property taxes in Orange Beach will drive up property values, igniting growth in the local real estate market. The time to press the advantage is now, because eventually Gulf Shores must raise property taxes, supporting an independent school system, driving up the demand for real estate in tax-free Orange Beach, creating wealth for local residents.

This idea embraces conservative ideology, but Mayor Tony Kennon will not support a tax cut. Rebating money to residents as shareholders is not what he does, and there is no way to change it.

In all fairness we should present practical arguments against tax cuts. Orange Beach must keep adding to its large reserves as a built-in cushion against the devastating effects of possible storms, keeping the city safe during the long recovery.

The downside is the Fed will look at Orange Beach's balance sheet after a disaster, having $40 million in reserves, arguing we don't need Federal Grants, passing the recovery funds on to more needy neighbors like Gulf Shores, Foley, Satsuma, Citronelle, Bon Secour, Bayou La Batre, and the Gulf State Park. You get penalized for running it like a business.

I argue a property tax repeal is necessary, giving back to the community, especially with a favorable balance sheet. Eliminating the 4-mil property tax is an opportunity, increasing real estate values, growing the economy, and creating wealth for local home owners.

15

THE PUPPY

L i'l Johny walked across the street, headed for the Backcountry Trail, crossing the park behind City Hall and in front of the Fire Station.

He enjoyed the beauty and sounds of the trail, wondering how the city was able to spare such prime real estate from development.

He turned right at the Tee, crossing the bridges, heading towards the Sportsplex.

Li'l Johny found a tree near the parking lot, climbed, waiting for his business meeting. He wanted get paid.

Li'l Johny awoke.

"What happened? How'd I get here?"

His legs and body were tied to a chair in the basement. The solitary light focused on him, the rest was dark. The place smelled of mold and urine.

"He's awake boss," said a voice to Li'l Johny's left, having a distinct northeastern accent.

"Make sure the effect of the dart has worn off."

Li'l Johny saw a glimpse of the gloved fist just before it pounded into his jaw, sending blood erupting from his mouth.

"Mr. HoHoHo is going to ask you some questions," said the gloved voice.

Pain sprouted like tendrils from Johnny's ear as he was hit again.

"Do you understand?"

Li'l Johny nodded his head, expecting to feel another blow.

From the darkness in front of him he saw the signature red linen pants and black cowboy boots of Mr. HoHoHo extend from the darkness. He spoke in a kinder voice.

"I gave you guys a job to do and you let me down," he said.

Behind him at the far end of the corridor Johnnie saw a door open and heard Billy whimpering before he was thrust into the light at Johnny's feet. He cried even more when he saw how pulverized Johnny's face looked.

The kinder voice explained, "You were supposed to pick up a puppy from the owner, bringing it across the line, and leaving it at a shop on Main Street, but the puppy never arrived," he paused, letting it sink in. "You see the puppy's collar has a USB drive sewn into it with all my bitcoin addresses and payments I received for delivering presents across the line."

"Do you understand me?" he asked.

Li'l Johny saw the gloved fist rise and shook his head yes.

"I know Billy here is deaf and dumb. The two of you use sign language to talk to each other since you were kids, and I want you to ask your friend or should I say your boyfriend," drawing laughter from several others in the room. "What he did with the puppy."

They cut Li'l Johny's hands free and he signed Billy asking him what he did with the puppy.

He replied.

Mr. HoHoHo asked, "What did he say?"

He said he picked up the puppy, drove across the line and gave it to the lady in the shop.

The pain stung in Johnnie's ear as the gloved fist crashed into his jaw. He thought he swallowed a tooth.

Li'l Johny recognized him from the Council Chambers.

Mr. HoHoHo took a pistol. Johnny saw him chamber a round, and HoHoHo asked, "What did he do with the puppy?" The barrel was pressed against Billy's temple. The hammer was back. Billy was on his knees, crying uncontrollably.

He signed, asking the question.

Billy replied, "I am so sorry. I hid the puppy in the old tunnel where we used to play as kids; he has lots of food and water. I barricaded him in.

"What did he say?" asked Mr. HoHoHo.

Li'l Johny said, "He doesn't believe you'll pull the trigger."

❧ 16 ❧

TAX RETURN DISCLOSURE FOR CANDIDATES

C ampaign finance is a fluid topic, cascading down from the Oval Office to the smallest hamlet, affecting every facet of political life. Alabama's Fair Campaign Practices Act (FCPA) is our guiding light.

Financial disclosures are mandatory. In 2018, when Orange Beach Councilman Jeff Boyd ran for the Alabama State Senate, and Councilman Jerry Johnson ran for Baldwin County Commissioner they filed reports with the Alabama Secretary of State's Office. Unfortunately, both campaigns flamed out in the Republican Primary.

Still they raised significant amounts of money through small donors, according to the search results, but Alabama has different rules for corporate contributions. "22 states completely prohibit corporations from contributing to political campaigns. Another six-Alabama, Missouri, Nebraska, Oregon, Utah, and Virginia-allow corporations to contribute an unlimited amount of money to state campaigns," according to a report on the National Conference of State Legislators website.

"As of May 2015, individuals, corporations, and unions in Alabama could make unlimited contributions to [municipal] candidates, PACs [political action committee that basically collects campaign contributions], party committees, legislative caucus committees, and ballot measure campaigns. Super PACs [independent-expenditure only committees] could not make direct contributions to the aforementioned individuals and groups," according to a report on Ballotopedia.

What rules govern campaign finance in Orange Beach?

"Candidates for municipal office are required to file disclosure reports in the same manner as state and county candidates. But, municipal candidates must file with the judge of probate in their county instead of filing electronically with the Secretary of State," said Clay Helms, Director of Elections, Alabama Secretary of State's Office in an email.

I reached out to the Judge of Probate's Office in Baldwin County for comment, but received a reference instead. "You should be able to go on the Probate website and...all the [municipal candidate] reports should come up," said Violetta Smith, Election Manager for Baldwin County Probate in an email.

To improve transparency, there is no law insisting candidates release their tax returns, according to the Alabama Fair Campaign Practices Act . I argue tax returns help provide openness, essentially guarding against conflicts of interest in a small town like Orange Beach.

Basically, we see all the rules for campaign finance disclosure are consistent across the state, requiring all candidates for public office to explain where the funds are coming from except when dealing with out-of-state monies. These are exempt from the local rules, "The Secretary of State's website says that federal PACs [Political Action Committees] aren't subject to Alabama law." according to a report on AL.com.

Running for public office requires research. Information regarding candidate filing requirements can be obtained from the Alabama Secretary of State's office.

This all sounds easy, but you need to design a plan: Know your electorate; connect with bellwethers; kick off fundraising; build your team; rent office space; hire staff like Campaign Manager, Treasurer and Field Director; design campaign material, raise candidate profile; create a campaign plan; paperwork to run; voter file for communication;

website, social media, and lots of volunteers, according to a report on CallHub.

Fundraising is a political art form. "Create a host committee of well-connected and enthusiastic individuals who are willing to promote your events [fundraisers] in the community," according to a report on NGPVAN. In 2018, Orange Beach Councilman Jeff Boyd ran against Baldwin County Commissioner Chris Elliot for the same seat in the Alabama State Senate. Elliot raised seven times more money than Boyd. Guess who won? In Alabama politics, money matters.

Money and politics did not always share the same bed. "The idea of candidates asking for contributions to fund their campaigns was completely foreign to George Washington. George and friends [the founders] probably would have been averse to political ads, directly soliciting donations from constituents, or accepting large sums of money from business PACs," according to a report on OpenSecrets.

Still this is the world we live in, especially in the mega-donor era. Digital campaigns, data analysis and constant polling, interpreting the results and re-polling are very expensive. The fundraising arm should be any candidate's most important operational focus.

I encourage qualified candidates to consider running, putting their names into the hat. In Orange Beach, the jobs of Mayor and City Councilman do not pay much, purposely set low, discouraging competition at the ballot box. The upside is council members have immense power over local decisions like what gets built where, building codes, flood-zone regulations, developing municipal real estate, spending grant monies from the BP Oil Spill, and employee benefits.

The candidate's reasons for running are ideally the desire to make a difference. To win organizing an efficient fundraising apparatus is essential, emulating the example of Alabama State Senator Chris Elliot, winning a seat in the Alabama State Senate.

Campaign finance disclosure is important, separating business from government, unmasking the underlying financial machinery. I argue for having each municipal candidate in Orange Beach release their personal and business tax returns as a vehicle for clarity, being as informative to voters as having them release the results of their drug test.

❧ 17 ❧

HARASSMENT CASE

Li'l Johny felt lucky to be alive. He'd done what he was told, and still hadn't been paid. "Damn," he thought.

A girl in her 20s was sitting on the trail bench, as he walked towards her. She was crying.

"What's wrong?" he asked.

"Never mind, I don't even know you."

"Sometimes it is easier to talk to people you don't know."

She paused, wiping her eyes.

"I work for the city. They hired someone in my department who sexually harassed me."

"Did you report it?" he asked.

"Yes, I did but management put him on administrative leave for five months with full pay, probably waiting for things to blow over. Then they reinstated him to work with me."

Li'l Johny was shocked, especially with all the publicity from the "MeToo" movement.

"What are you going to do?" he asked.

"I guess like all the women before me, I will suffer in silence."

She got up, walking towards the Sportsplex.

SOLUTIONISM

S olutionists believe their way is the only way, fighting against the tide of possibilities, reasoning they have thought the problem through, analyzed all the facts, and concluded their vision is completely correct.

Orange Beach Mayor Tony Kennon is a solutionist. He espouses the fix to the traffic problem in Orange Beach is more roads and bridges to move the tourists, ignoring the evidence that unbridled development on the beach road caused the problem, and it happened over the last ten years on his watch.

We are past the point of limiting development, but not past the point of asking ourselves if this government is governed by council's addiction to the wealth from tourism, or if the notion of maintaining our small-town quality of life means more to us than supporting council's devotion to increasing the city's tax yield on revenues. The unfolding rests with voting for council seats in 2020, possibly giving birth to a group of neomillennial politicians.

Solutionism is singularly focused on the distillation of one person's ideas, letting them implement every policy of government in a democracy. This requires the collective surrender of all the levers of power, believing the strong individual understands the big picture better than anyone else in the community. The mayor and council are not co-equal branches of government as defined by the founders.

Mayor Kennon is the person we elected to lead us through the very difficult recession of 2008, recovering from the post-Ivan devastation of 2005. In 2018 our town sits with cash reserves of more than $40 million, according to documents on the city's web site.

This is commendable, and I am thankful for the city's fiscal solvency, providing job security for municipal employees.

Perhaps it is time to plan for a change away from solutionism. The Alabama Constitution Section 2 provides guidance, "That all political power is inherent in the people, and all free governments are founded on their authority, and instituted for their benefit; and that, therefore, they have at all times an inalienable and indefeasible right to change their form of government in such manner as they may deem expedient," according to a report on Justia (https://law.justia.com/constitution/alabama/CA-245533.html).

Districting Council Seats is one alternative, forcing each council member to support the concerns of their constituents, not the vision of the strong mayor.

Mayor Tony Kennon went on a lobbying tour in January of this year, visiting Rotary Clubs and Chambers across the state, arguing for a transportation solution through the State Park (Powerline Road), even though the BP Agreement prohibited such an environmentally destructive project for two decades.

"A federal lawsuit that was settled last year, and which enabled a new beachside conference center and hotel complex to move forward, bluntly declares that no north-south connecting road [Powerline Road] can be built through a popular coastal Alabama state park for the next 20 years," according to a report by John Sharp at al.com (https://www.al.com/news/beaches/2018/11/mayor-pitches-north-south-beach-road-but-federal-settlement-may-prevent-it.html).

The solutionist in Kennon rails against this part of the settlement.

According to a report by John Mullen in the Lagniappe, "I really want to start educating these folks to just how simple the fix is, and that is the road down Powerline Road [north-south corridor] to the beach," Kennon said. "It could solve so many of our traffic problems during the summer. I'm going to start beating that drum now all over the state as we need help getting that done."

Kennon continues, "These are Alabama's beaches, we're the stewards of them and you guys need to help us build the infrastructure and maintain the infrastructure that we need to move all these tourists. You're not doing Orange Beach a favor by helping us out, you're doing the state of Alabama a service because there's so much money generated down here and a good bit of it goes to Montgomery. Orange Beach generates about 15 percent of all lodging tax in the state. This is significant."

Solutionism reflected in Mayor Tony Kennon's words speaks volumes. This key issue neglects to mention who will get the bill for breaking the BP Agreement, building a road across the state park.

Alabama should not entertain paying for nonsense in Orange Beach, including the proposed Flyover Bridge west of the Foley Beach Express. Confiscating properties through eminent domain to build this bridge rails against conservative values. Nothing says socialism quite like seizing private lands.

Orange Beach boasts overflowing coffers, enthusiastically campaigning against preserving the environmental integrity of the state park, but still grabbing their portion of the BP settlement, "We were very pleased with $40 million, with $275 million on the table, I've seen knifing's and shootings for a whole lot less but it was fairly distributed and very equitable," Kennon said, according to a report on Fox10 News.

Solutionism is driving the conversation in Orange Beach. We see diametrically opposing forces at work here, simultaneously wanting to kill the BP Settlement, proposing a road across the state park, and concurrently blessing the BP Settlement monies the city has yet to receive.

Perhaps it is time to reflect.

❧ 19 ❧

LI'L JOHNY'S RIDE

Li'l Johny called the lady who gave him a ride into Orange Beach.

"The conference is finished. My husband and the kids just left. Come over for a drink."

He started walking.

AFTERWORD

Thank you for buying my book and reading it all the way to the end.

If you have a moment could you please leave a review, following this link:

http://humorousincidentsshortstoriesandessays.com.

Also, please sign up for my newsletter: http://raufbolden.com.

Your feedback is helpful for me, and other potential readers.

Thanks again!

ABOUT THE AUTHOR

We are adventurers. Starting in 1984, my wife Jeannette Dean and I sailed around the world in a 35 ft. fiberglass sloop, seeing and experiencing places and people we will never forget. It is this love of people, striving to make the world a better place on a global scale that motivated me to write this book.

We do not live on an island. We represent humanity at large. To this end, I learned German, French, and Dutch, giving me more insight into and appreciation of cultural diversity.

I am an emerging author of political essays, having been published in myriad online magazines. This is my first book.

Recently retired as IT Director at the City of Orange Beach in Alabama, I am presently working as an IT & Web Technologies Consultant on the Beach Road. Please contact me by email: helpdesk@raufbolden.com. or visit my author's website: http://raufbolden.com.